Play Foundations

Exploring My World

Dr Hannah Mortimer

Acknowledgements

United Kingdom: Folens Publishers, Waterslade House, Thame Road, Haddenham, Buckinghamshire HP17 8NT.
Email: folens@folens.com

Ireland: Folens Publishers, Greenhills Road, Tallaght, Dublin 24.
Email: info@folens.ie

Commissioning Editor: Zoë Nichols
Illustrations: Graeme Holding
Design and layout: Infuze Ltd
Managing editor: Jane Morgan
Cover illustration: Cathy Hughes
Cover design: Infuze Ltd

With thanks to the following for their permission to use poems and extracts:
All Development matters statements and Aspects of learning quoted in this book are taken from *Practice Guidance for the Early Years Foundation Stage* (Department for Education and Skills) and are reproduced under the terms of the Click-Use Licence.

First published 2008 by Folens Limited.

Every effort has been made to contact copyright holders of material used in this publication. If any copyright holder has been overlooked, we should be pleased to make any necessary arrangements.

British Library Cataloguing in Publication Data. A catalogue record for this publication is available from the British Library.

ISBN 978-1-85008-341-2

Contents

Introduction

Who the book is for

This book forms part of the *Play Foundations* series which provides guidance for practitioners in setting up quality play scenarios or activities with young children. It is written for all those who work with children under three in a whole range of early years settings – in the private, voluntary and independent sectors and in Children's Centres. The activities will also adapt easily for childminders working at home. It will be of special interest to all those who are working within the Early Years Foundation Stage framework (EYFS) and, of course, to parents*.

Learning through play

The activities in this book are based on the EYFS principles:

- Each child is unique and is a competent learner from birth.
- Positive relationships ensure that children learn to be strong and independent.
- Enabling environments play a key role in extending learning and development.
- Learning and development takes many different forms and all areas are connected.

You will find that the focus of the activities is on child-initiated learning and that the emphasis is on process rather than product. There are suggestions for using your guidance, your language and your support to promote the children's learning within the EYFS framework as they explore and play. Many of the activities can be enjoyed outside or inside. Being outdoors has a positive impact on children's sense of well-being and can help all aspects of development.

How to use this book

The book is divided into five chapters, each focusing on different ways in which children can enjoy and learn from 'exploring my world'. The chapters are:

- Using my senses
- Messy play
- What's outside?
- Colours and shapes
- Materials.

The activities

Each chapter has seven or eight activities including ideas for children of 0–11 months; 8–0 months; 16–26 months and 22–36 months. Some of the activities are designed for small groups of children and others are for use when you are working individually with a child.

Each activity is divided into the following sections:

- To help to plan *Enabling environments,* there is a section on *Setting up,* outlining the resources needed.
- *Getting started* describes how to organise the actual activity.

- *Let's talk!* provides ideas for talking with the children about their experiences, including questions that can be asked and how to differentiate language to suit the children's varying abilities. There are also suggestions for making the most of assessment opportunities.
- Recognising *A unique child and Positive relationships* means making sure that self-esteem, confidence and relationships remain positive and there is a *Top tip* for doing so.
- The *Differentiation* section includes ideas for personalising the learning by adjusting each activity to make it easier for those children needing support or more challenging for others. This section will also be useful for planning inclusive activities for those children who have special or additional needs.
- *Further ideas* for each activity suggest ways of extending and enhancing learning and development opportunities.

How to support children as they learn

Supporting the children's learning means setting up positive interactions and listening to what the children have to tell you, with their voices, their reactions or their behaviour. Whatever stage a child has reached in their communication, they need space and time to respond to people, things and events around them and to know that practitioners are giving their full attention and encouragement. Spend a few seconds simply observing a child before moving in to interact, so that you can tune in to what they are doing, thinking about or reflecting upon at that moment.

Effective teaching means systematically helping children to learn so that they make connections in their learning – this involves knowing when to stand back as well as when to step in. Practitioners need to get to know each individual child well so they can judge the best kind of support and know when the child is ready to learn new skills. The use of the key person system allows children to form secure attachments and, from this sense of security, feel confident to explore and to develop further. The key person is the member of staff with whom the child has most contact and who shows special interest in the child through close interaction.

Working with parents

The EYFS emphasises that when parents and practitioners work together in early years settings, the results have a positive impact on children's development and learning. As you make progress through these activities, share your observations regularly with parents so that you can learn from each other. Newsletters, home-setting diaries and displays are all useful methods for doing this, making sure that everyone feels welcomed and included, that you respect diversity and that you communicate in ways that are accessible for everyone.

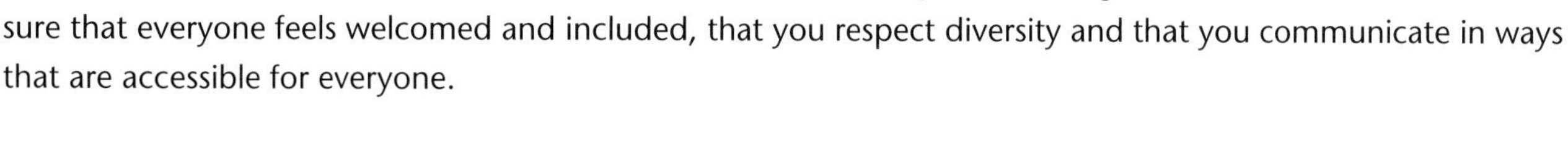

* Whenever the term 'parent' is used this is taken to include parents and/or the children's primary carers.

Planning chart

Use this chart to help with your planning. Each activity focuses on either one or two Area(s) of learning and development. These are highlighted by the stars shown on the chart. The Areas of learning and development are divided up into 'aspects' and the aspect(s) for each activity are also provided on the chart. On the activity pages you will also find a 'Development matters' objective for each activity.

The following key is used on the activity pages.

PSED: Personal, social and emotional development

KUW: Knowledge and understanding of the world

CLL: Communication, language and literacy

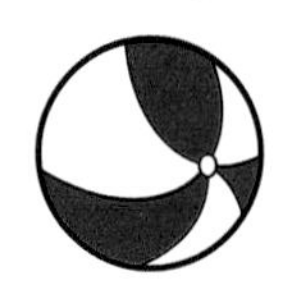

PD: Physical development

PSRN: Problem solving, reasoning and numeracy

CD: Creative development

Activities	Areas of learning and development								
Using my senses	**Page**	**Age**	**PSED**	**CLL**	**PSRN**	**KUW**	**PD**	**CD**	**Aspect of learning**
Watch me!	10	0–11 months				★			Exploration and investigation
Reaching out	11	0–11 months					★		Using equipment and materials
						★			Exploration and investigation
Is it a bird?	12	8–20 months		★					Linking sounds and letters
Sounds good	13	8–20 months						★	Being creative – responding to experiences, expressing and communicating ideas
The hunting game	14	16–26 months					★		Movement and space
						★			Exploration and investigation
Wrap it up	15	16–26 months			★				Shape, space and measures
Little musicians	16	22–36 months						★	Creating music and dance
Smellies and tasties	17	22–36 months		★					Language for thinking
								★	Being creative – responding to experiences, expressing and communicating ideas
Messy play	**Page**	**Age**	**PSED**	**CLL**	**PSRN**	**KUW**	**PD**	**CD**	**Aspect of learning**
Happy splashing	18	0–11 months					★		Movement and space
						★			Exploration and investigation
Fingers in!	19	0–11 months						★	Exploring media and materials
			★						Self-care
Mirror art	20	8–20 months						★	Exploring media and materials
				★					Language for thinking
Jelly wobble	21	8–20 months						★	Developing imagination and imaginative play
Messy play day	22	16–26 months					★		Movement and space
Mud pies	23	16–26 months				★			Exploration and investigation
							★		Using equipment and materials

	Page	Age	PSED	CLL	PSRN	KUW	PD	CD	Aspect of learning
Buried treasure	24	22–36 months						★	Developing imagination and imaginative play
				★					Language for thinking
Splat pictures	25	22–36 months						★	Exploring media and materials
						★			Designing and making
What's outside?	**Page**	**Age**	**PSED**	**CLL**	**PSRN**	**KUW**	**PD**	**CD**	
Cherry blossom	26	0–11 months						★	Being creative – responding to experiences, expressing and communicating ideas
The watching window	27	0–11 months				★			Exploration and investigation
Picnic time	28	8–20 months	★						Self-care
Rain and shine	29	8–20 months				★			Exploration and investigation
					★				Numbers as labels and for counting
Outdoor clothes	30	16–26 months	★						Behaviour and self-control
			★						Self-care
Out and about	31	16–26 months		★					Reading
						★			Exploration and investigation
The great outdoors	32	22–36 months					★		Movement and space
Outside memories	33	22–36 months				★			Time
Colours and shapes	**Page**	**Age**	**PSED**	**CLL**	**PSRN**	**KUW**	**PD**	**CD**	
Look closely	34	0–11 months				★			ICT
Yoo-hoo!	35	0–11 months						★	Being creative – responding to experiences, expressing and communicating ideas
					★				Shape, space and measures
Rollaround	36	8–20 months					★		Movement and space
Surprise surprise!	37	8–20 months	★						Dispositions and attitudes
					★				Shape, space and measures
Same and different	38	16–26 months			★				Calculating
Solid sort-out	39	16–26 months				★			Designing and making
Shape hunt	40	22–36 months		★					Language for thinking
The colour game	41	22–36 months						★	Creating music and dance
							★		Movement and space
Materials	**Page**	**Age**	**PSED**	**CLL**	**PSRN**	**KUW**	**PD**	**CD**	
Paper fun	42	0–11 months						★	Being creative – responding to experiences, expressing and communicating ideas
Reach and swipe	43	0–11 months				★			Exploration and investigation
							★		Using equipment and materials
What's in the box?	44	8–20 months			★				Calculating
Mega art	45	8–20 months					★		Using equipment and materials
								★	Exploring media and materials
Collage and chat	46	16–26 months	★						Dispositions and attitudes
				★					Language for thinking
Fresh bread rolls	47	16–26 months				★			Time
							★		Using equipment and materials
It's your choice	48	22–36 months						★	Exploring media and materials

Assessment ideas

Babies and young children are individuals first, each with a unique profile of abilities. All the planning that we do should flow from the observations that we make on an ongoing basis and these will help us to understand and consider their current interests, development and learning.

How to assess children

Observing children during their daily routines allows us to note their responses in different situations and to different people. In some settings, a specific Area of learning and development is targeted and the key person is asked to observe what stage the children in their care have reached over the next day or week, revisiting that Area from time to time. Others use sticky notes in order to capture relevant observations and record significant times for a child's learning or evidence of new understanding. These can be collated later by a key person and entered into the ongoing records for the child. Others still make use of photos, daily diaries, activity feedback sheets or tracking records to capture the children's progress at different times. There is no prescribed method and practitioners find methods that suit their practice and the children and families concerned.

Planning for assessment

Through assessment you can see what stages the children have reached in their learning and development and therefore work out the best resources, opportunities and activities to plan next. Sometimes this might involve planning a specific activity to enable the children to take their learning that little bit further. Sometimes it will simply mean providing opportunities and observing the children as they play and learn independently. You will find a mixture of adult-led and child-led activities in this book. Suggestions for you to observe and assess the children are given within the *Let's talk!* sections.

Using your assessments

Once you have observed the children at play, analyse your observations and highlight the children's achievements or their need for further support. Involve parents as part of the ongoing observation and assessment process and share your plans for the short-term (a week) and long-term (a term) planning. Your planning should always follow the same pattern – observe, analyse and reflect, then use what you have found out to plan next steps in the child's learning. In this way you can personalise the children's learning and make the most of their strengths, interests and needs.

The 'Look, listen and note' approach of the EYFS is a helpful tool when deciding what and how to observe. On the next page, this format has been applied to children 'exploring my world' so that you can begin to think about how your assessment and observations of children within this theme can feed back into your planning.

Observation hints

Here are some suggestions to help you focus your observations and assessments when supporting children who are 'exploring my world'.

Chapter heading	Look, listen and note
Using my senses	Record evidence of babies turning towards sights and sounds. Note the stage at which they begin to make sense of that information – looking round for someone or reaching for a toy. Write down the responses children make to different things they see, hear or touch and what preferences they develop. Quote snapshots of how children repeat play patterns as they explore with their various senses.
Messy play	Capture in photos when babies first begin to make smears and marks on wet or messy surfaces. Observe the responses of children to the different messy play resources they encounter and any language they use. Keep photographic evidence or examples of creations and involve the children in deciding what to celebrate in this way.
What's outside?	Monitor children's play and make sure that they have a balance of indoor and outdoor experiences. Note the children's choices and preferred outdoor play and learning activities. Help children collect their own 'evidence' (such as photos) of what they have experienced and achieved outside.
Colours and shapes	Note down babies' responses to brightly coloured objects and playthings. Record the vocabulary children use spontaneously when interacting with colours and shapes. Use photos to capture special moments in children's understanding of colour and shape, such as a clever pattern or sequence they have produced; a simple construction made out of 3D shapes or a spontaneous matching of like or contrasting colours.
Materials	Observe and record how babies move their bodies in response to different materials around them. Note the connections children make when exploring materials – how they use one material in conjunction with another to explore with or to achieve a purpose. Record samples of the children's vocabulary as they explore and interact with a range of materials.

Using my senses Watch me!

Age range: 0–11 months

Here are some ideas for hiding and seeking which encourage babies to look around them and show curiosity about what might happen next.

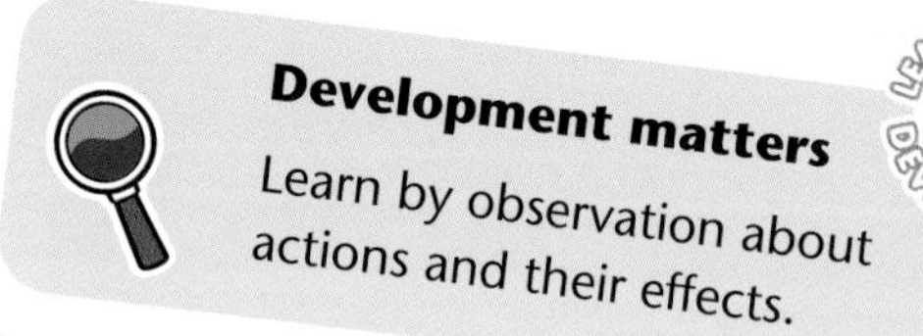

Development matters

Learn by observation about actions and their effects.

Setting up

Wait for the right moment and make use of whatever is available – cushions, scarves, a tea towel, your hands or even the furniture and fittings! These ideas are best from around two months onwards and are useful for indoors or out.

Getting started

- Wait until the baby is alert and interested. Start by talking gently and making eye contact together. Once you have lots of smiling and chuckling, pop your face out of view for a moment as you say, for example *Where's Jade?* then reappear with a gentle *Boo!*
- Duck behind a cushion when you are on the floor; stoop down beside the cot after rest time; peep round a door or cover your face with your hands at the snack table. The idea is to hold the baby's attention until you reappear again. This shows very clever 'baby thinking' as you are engaging both their curiosity and attention and proving that you continue to exist even if you cannot be seen!
- Now try hiding your faces with chiffon scarves and drawing the scarves away again – both your own and the baby's.
- Try drawing along a stringed toy or rolling a large ball behind a box and causing it to reappear again. At first, the baby will continue to look where it disappeared, though later they will move their eyes to focus on where it is due to reappear again.

Let's talk!

Keep your commentary going while you hide. This way you are providing reassurance and holding the baby's attention. Provide support by asking, for example, *Where's Emma?* Challenge babies by calling out from your hiding place, *Junaid, where am I?* and then reappear into view. Observe the baby as you reappear and note whether they are surprised (first stage for younger babies) or anticipating you (next stage for older babies).

Top tip

Observe the stage at which the baby is no longer surprised when you reappear again.This shows that they are now beginning to anticipate how objects in their world behave. Using light scarves usually prevents any anxiety, though never cover faces unless the baby enjoys the game.

Differentiation

This activity can be enjoyed at all levels and encourages an important stage in development, understanding that things continue to exist even when you cannot see them. Challenge children by asking them to find toys that you hide for them, holding their attention on that toy until it comes back into their sight.

Further ideas

- Encourage the older babies to put toys in and out of plastic tubs.
- Hide toys in simple boxes to be rediscovered again.

Reaching out

Age range: 0–11 months

Teaching babies to reach out and touch is so easy – just provide something safe and interesting to catch their attention and watch them learn!

Development matters

Reach out for, touch and begin to hold objects.

Use movement and senses to focus on, reach for and handle objects.

Setting up

Look around your play areas (outdoors as well as in) and suspend various mobiles and objects to twist and turn at shoulder height for yourself. Make sure they can all be safely reached out for, swiped or even grasped by little fingers. Arrange small and colourful toys and safe playthings on various surfaces (again about at your own shoulder height) so make use of the tops of cupboards and shelves. As before, choose objects and toys that can be safely swiped or reached for such a soft toys, rattles, plastic cups and bright scarves.

Getting started

- Carry the babies in turn as you go for an expedition around your play surfaces. Stop to look at various toys and objects of interest. Pause beneath a turning mobile or set a wind chime in motion with your hand as you pass.
- Focus the babies' attention on the items of interest and encourage the babies to reach out towards or even grasp objects as you move around.

Let's talk!

Provide a simple commentary as you explore the objects together. Provide support by pausing for the babies to respond in between your words and echo back the sounds they are making. Challenge the babies by drawing their attention to the toys and objects around them by using your voice, their name and moving the object to attract their attention. *Look, Dan – a bird – see it turn!* Observe each baby's response to the colours, textures and shapes and whether they reach out for, touch or handle what they see.

Top tip

Some babies are very sensitive to different kinds of touch. Help them feel less aroused by introducing a range of textures to their hands and cheeks and playing gently with them.

Differentiation

Make this easy by placing the baby beneath a 'baby gym' (or make your own by suspending a number of baby toys from a light frame within reach of the babies when lying on their backs). Make it harder by encouraging the babies to reach into a box or container to pick up a toy.

Further ideas

- Hold the babies underneath the waving blossom branches of a fruit tree in spring, or suspend ribbons and scarves from a fence to blow and flutter in the wind. Encourage the babies to reach towards the colours.

Is it a bird?

Age range: 8–20 months

As babies develop, they can begin to recognise familiar objects when they are partly hidden. Here is an activity all about looking.

Setting up

Make a list of the child's early words (these can be real words or those that are personal to the child, such as *dodo* for dummy). Some of these will be words for familiar toys or objects. Gather a few of these objects together and place them in a box.

Development matters

Enjoy babbling and increasingly experiment with using sounds and words to represent objects around them.

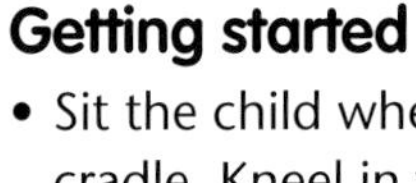

Getting started

- Sit the child where they can see you easily, in a chair or cradle. Kneel in front of them with the box on your knee. Make a game of attracting the child's attention to what you have in the box. Slowly draw one of the objects out so that the child can only see part of it at a time. Say, *Look – it's Ted …* Pause and smile to see if the child responds with the word. If not, repeat it for them, *It's Teddy!*
- Give Teddy to the child to play with for a few moments and then draw attention to your next item using the same approach. If the child comes out with the initial sound or the word itself, cheer and make a big fuss.

Let's talk!

Continue to play with the items at the end and label each as the child picks it up. *You've got the cup now – where's the spoon? Is it Jem's hat? Is it a book? No – it's Panda!* To provide support, try providing just the first sound of an item at other times during the session when the child is attempting to label something. Challenge children by using sentence completion, *What's this? It's …* Keep a note of new sounds and words that the children use when playing this game and at other times too.

Top tip

This activity really encourages early memory and recognition skills; not only does the child have to solve the mystery of something partly hidden but also the mystery of something partly spoken. Keep it fun and inspire confidence!

Differentiation

Make this activity easier by introducing just two items. Spend time before using the box simply showing the items and labelling them. Then ask, *Where's Teddy*? Where's the *cup*? Make the activity more difficult by inviting the child to combine two items together when you play with all the items at the end – *Give Teddy the spoon! Roll the ball to Panda!*

Further ideas

- Collect family photos – if these are digital, enlarge and edit them so that each photo is a full face. Hide them in a shoe box and draw them out gradually as you discover who it is – *It's Da …Daddy*!

Sounds good

Age range: 8–20 months

Here is a game for helping young children locate and turn towards sounds to help them develop good listening skills.

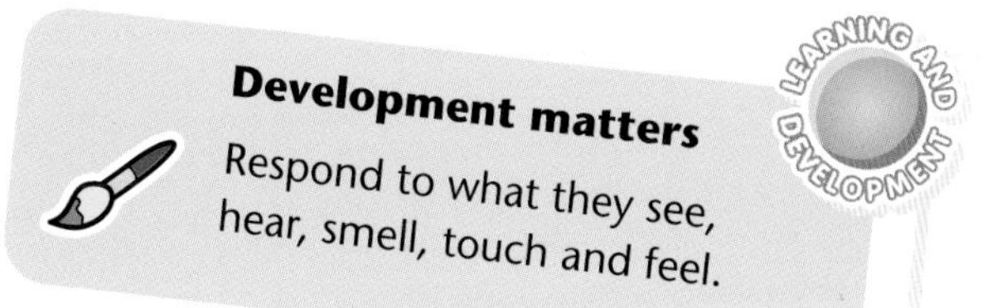

Setting up

Gather the helpers and children in a circle so that the children are sitting propped between the adults' knees on the floor. Arrange for your two extra helpers to stand or kneel up opposite each other in the circle. Give each helper two or three instruments, such as a tambourine, a shaker, some bells and some castanets.

Getting started

- The first helper should show their first instrument and attract the children's attention to it by shaking or beating it. The helper then holds the instrument behind their back so that it is now out of view. The second helper should do the same with their first instrument. Each time, encourage the children to turn and look towards where the sound is coming from.
- The helpers then wink at each other in order to agree who goes first. One of them makes a sound with the instrument behind their backs, as everyone encourages the children to *listen!* and keeps quiet for them to do so. Continue until each instrument has been played once or twice.
- Finish by letting the children have fun exploring the instruments themselves!

Let's talk!

Say, *Look! Sarah has some bells and they sound like this! But she's going to hide them …listen! Where's the sound?* Offer support by asking, *Were you right? Let's see …* (revealing the instrument and cheering enthusiastically!). Offer challenge by naming the instrument and asking the children to locate it, *Where are the bells?* The adult playing the sound will be in a unique position to observe which of the children are looking or turning towards the sound and which are not. Be alert for any children who might have a difficulty in hearing sounds – this might be a sign of hearing loss, perhaps associated with colds or ear infections.

Top tip

By slowly revealing the hidden sound, the helpers are encouraging all the children to feel successful – there is no 'right' and 'wrong' involved. Praising and encouraging the children in this way will help to build your positive relationship with them.

Differentiation

Make this activity simpler by using one instrument and sounding it to one side, encouraging the children to turn and look for the sound. Make it harder by asking children to point and by introducing three extra helpers at different points of the circle.

Further ideas

- Use as feely bag to hide noise-making toys and instruments. Encourage the children to feel them and then have a look inside to hear what is making the sound. Some children may be able to identify what they can hear, *Duck!* or *Rattle!*

The hunting game

Age range: 16–26 months

Here is a toddler version of a treasure hunt to encourage looking and listening.

Development matters

Are excited by their own increasing mobility and often set their own challenges.

Sometimes focus their enquiries on particular features or processes.

Setting up

Gather together three or four musical boxes or wind-up/electronic musical toys.

Getting started

- Show the children your musical items and enjoy listening to their sounds together. Introduce one at a time so that their sounds are distinct and can be heard easily.
- While one adult distracts the children, another should hide one of the musical toys somewhere where it can be easily heard and found by the children, perhaps underneath a light cover or behind a teddy bear.
- Go for a toddle with the children as you move around your space and listen for the sound. Celebrate as you find the toy and repeat for the other musical items until the children begin to anticipate the game.
- Now hide the items in your outdoor space, perhaps round a corner or behind a plant pot, and set off their sounds. Go for a toddle out of doors and pause to listen for the sounds as you get closer to each one. See if you can locate them all!

Let's talk!

Ask, *Where's the sound? Can you find it? Is it under/behind/on top of the slide?* To provide support, keep your language simple as you emphasise the key words associated with hiding, seeking and position. Provide extension by giving children simple instructions to help you hide the sound, *Can you put it under the bush?* Take your lead from the children and observe how well they can each hear and locate sounds. Observe each child's curiosity – can they, with your encouragement, keep their minds on the game and continue until the musical items are found?

Top tip

Make sure that you keep this game easy enough and brief enough for all the children you are working with to be able to concentrate and to succeed. Success breeds confidence and they will be more ready to look and listen to you next time.

Differentiation

Make this game easier by hiding one musical box beneath one of two light cushions. Make it more complex by making it harder to see the musical toys and gradually reducing the amount of help you give the children.

Further ideas

- Play a version of the traditional game 'Hunt the thimble' by hiding Teddy and singing (to the tune of 'Auld Lang Syne') *How warm you are, how warm you are, How warm you are, How warm* … louder and louder as a child gets closer to where Teddy is hidden.

Wrap it up

Age range: 16–26 months

You don't need to wait for a special occasion to enjoy wrapping and unwrapping surprises!

Development matters
Enjoy filling and emptying containers.

Setting up

Collect together plenty of old gift wrapping paper, some assorted cardboard boxes and cartons, sticky tape and a selection of favourite toys and everyday items.

Getting started

- Wrap up several toys and items in wrapping paper, fastening it loosely with sticky tape and leaving plenty of loose flaps for little fingers to get inside and rip. Place some of the items into boxes (with loose flaps) or cartons (open-topped) before wrapping.
- Arrange all the surprises in the centre of the carpet or on a mat outside. Share the fun as the children begin to open the parcels and discover what is inside. Encourage the children to look, feel and listen as they handle the wrappings. Encourage them as they continue to play with the items and the paper, placing them in and out of the wrappers and containers or crinkling the paper to make interesting sights and sounds.
- Be there to add a small length of sticky tape if the children try to wrap the items up again. Play a game of giving and receiving parcels from each other. Enjoy a rummage beneath all the paper as you hide from each other. Look for other things to wrap up and open again!
- For the next few sessions, arrange for there to be a few surprises to be opened and discovered each day. Encourage the children to hunt for the parcels and enjoy handling and unwrapping them.

Let's talk!

As you pass parcels to each other, encourage the children with an exaggerated *please* and *thank you.* Support children by saying, for example, *Leo, here you are.* Use the words *look, listen* and *feel* as you encourage the children to use their senses. Make your language more challenging by introducing position words, *What's inside?* Observe the point at which each child becomes more curious about discovering the contents than distracted by the wrappers.

Top tip

Children soon learn to behave in different ways in different situations. If a child is tempted to rip the pages of a picture book, point out that they can't rip the book but they can rip one of your surprise parcels open instead – have one handy 'just in case'.

Differentiation

Keep this simple by loosely wrapping a Teddy or bulky soft toy. Make this harder by wrapping a selection of uniquely shaped items and challenging children to use sight and touch to find the car and so on.

Further ideas

- Have fun wrapping up the toddler slide or climbing frame loosely with old gift-wrap. Leave it in its usual place. *What could it be?* Can the children find out?

Little musicians

Age range: 22–36 months

Music can be enjoyed at all ages and abilities and is a really useful way to help young children develop their senses of touching and listening.

Development matters

Create sounds by banging, shaking, tapping or blowing.

Setting up

- Put your existing instruments away and gather together a whole range of items that could, if experimented with, make interesting sounds. Empty plastic tubs and upturned buckets make excellent drums. Unused washing-up brushes, washing-up mops or wooden spoons make great beaters. Fill containers and packets with pulses and grains then seal them to create shakers. You also need a musical CD or tape.

Getting started

- Run your regular music time, but instead of your usual instruments, present the items you have collected and enjoy a 'jam session' as you experiment with new sounds and sound-making objects. As the children begin to beat, shake and strike; listen and copy each other until you have found a selection of sounds you enjoy.
- Now put on some music to make your sounds to, encouraging the children to experiment and move freely to the music. Share the fun with the children. Play when the accompaniment plays and stop when it stops.
- When you have finished your session, leave the sound-making items out so that the children can revisit them and experiment with new sounds. As always, supervise the children for safety, especially when they are experimenting with beaters.

Let's talk!

Draw the children's attention to what they are doing and what they can hear. Add your own describing words such as *loud, soft, gentle, fierce, quick*. Offer support by using the simple words, *Stop! Go!* as you play. Challenge the children by saying, *Can you make a loud noise? Can you play quickly?* Observe how flexibly the children can change between different items, finding new ways of making sounds.

Top tip

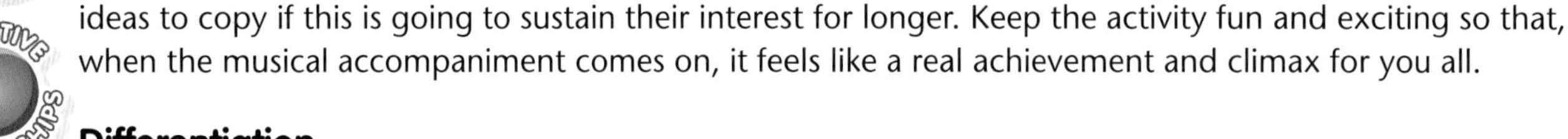

Sit back long enough for the children to do their own experimenting, but step in and offer them some ideas to copy if this is going to sustain their interest for longer. Keep the activity fun and exciting so that, when the musical accompaniment comes on, it feels like a real achievement and climax for you all.

Differentiation

Support children by suggesting that they beat a 'drum' with their hands or show them how to shake an item. Challenge children to experiment by combining different beaters and drum surfaces together.

Further ideas

- Encourage the children to clap hands or use their voices to make quiet sounds or loud sounds depending on how quietly or loudly you beat a drum. Children find this easiest if other adults are doing it too.

Smellies and tasties

Age range: 22–36 months

Try these lovely ideas for helping the children to explore the sense of smell.

Development matters

Use language as a powerful means of widening contacts, sharing feelings, experiences and thoughts.

Seek to make sense of what they see, hear, smell, touch and feel.

Setting up

Gather together a selection of sensory books (those with interesting textures and also scratch-and-smell pages if possible). Collect a selection of jars, little food containers (such as yoghurt pots), cotton wool balls and food items.

Getting started

- Think of a new smell each session to introduce to the children. As they arrive, for example, there could be the smell of fresh baking or you could have a bunch of sweet peas or a bowl of pot-pourri for them to sniff. Point out smells outside and introduce new fruity smells at snack time.
- Make special use of your regular cookery time to pause and appreciate the smells and how these change throughout the preparation and cooking.
- Introduce some sensory books into your book corner and support the children as they explore them with you.
- Soak cotton wool balls in some familiar foods, such as chocolate drink, orange, cinnamon, coffee and lemon juice. Place these in different jars with closed lids. Let the children open and explore these as you support them.
- Help the children to make up their own smelly jars or tasting boxes, using small jars, containers and food items. Be aware of any allergies or strong dislikes and make sure the smelly items do not get mistaken for food!

Let's talk!

Ask, *What can you smell? Do you like this one? Which one smells of banana?*
Offer support by asking, *Have you smelt this before?* Challenge the children by asking, *What does it smell like? What does it taste like?* Observe how ready each child is to experiment with tasting and smelling. Keep a note of any strong preferences or dislikes.

Top tip

Many children at this age have a very narrow range of food preferences. Introducing new tastes and smells in small doses can help them become more adventurous. Never force this activity – allow the children to go at their own paces so that they feel confident and in control.

Differentiation

Keep this simple by making sure a child can smell dinner and talk about it before it appears. Challenge children to tell you what different smells and tastes are, even if they cannot see the food.

Further ideas

- Introduce a new healthy snack item each day just to be sampled – such as two slices of banana sandwiched together with honey.

Messy play Happy splashing

Age range: 0–11 months

Here is an idea for setting up a dabbling pool – simply a younger version of a paddling pool!

Setting up

Find a large shallow tray that will not slip about on its surface, such as a plastic toy box lid with rounded edges or large plastic tea tray placed on to a non-slip mat.

Development matters

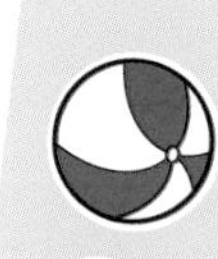

Use movement and sensory exploration to link up with their immediate environment.

Learn by observation about actions and their effects.

LEARNING AND DEVELOPMENT

Getting started

- Set up your shallow tray and non-slip surface in the wet area of your playroom or a suitable smooth area outside. Make sure the ambient temperature is warm enough for the babies to get wet. Add about one centimetre of lukewarm water. Carry out your usual risk assessments for safety and make sure there is one adult per baby.
- Remove most of the babies' clothing so that they are left with items that can easily become wet. Encourage the older babies to crawl up to and dabble their hands and feet, probably climbing right in as well!
- After a while, add some floating toys to add interest and encourage reaching out and touching. Support the younger babies in positions where they can feel the water and make movements in it. Share some quiet times together as you dry and change the babies afterwards.

Let's talk!

Name body parts as the babies move and interact with the water. Offer support by watching what they are doing and copying some of their actions, adding a simple commentary as you do so – *Jojo is wet! Look at your toes now!* Challenge the babies by making suggestions and modelling actions for them, *Can you splash?* Observe the babies' responses to the water and whether they are beginning to repeat actions and explore.

Top tip

Use your facial expressions and voice to hold the babies' attention and encourage their confidence. It is important that their early experiences with water should be as enjoyable and relaxing as possible.

Differentiation

Make this activity easier for younger babies by cradling them gently as you pour water over their toes or fingertips. Guide their hands gently to the water. Older babies might enjoy playing with foam – add some gentle baby bubble bath for extra interest. Do take care with children who have baby eczema – ask parents whether you need to do anything different from usual.

Further ideas

- This activity would lead well into a session using baby massage. Why not involve some of your parents and invite an expert along to demonstrate?

Fingers in!

Age range: 0–11 months

This activity recognises that you cannot separate early feeding from sensory play – so make the most of it!

Development matters

Discover mark-making by chance, noticing, for instance, that trailing a finger through spilt juice changes it.

Anticipate food routines with interest.

Setting up

Find duplicates of the normal spoons and plastic baby plates that you use. Plan ahead for any mess, cover carpets with a sheet and wear an apron yourself!

Getting started

- These ideas are suitable for babies who can sit up and are beginning to be fed with a spoon. As you feed the babies, place a second spoon in their hands. Encourage them to explore this as you feed them.
- Place a second baby dish on to their tray in front of them with just a small amount of the food on it. Use brightly coloured dishes and contrasting food to attract their attention. Allow the babies to explore this with fingers or dip the spoon into the food. Keep feeding the main part of the meal from your own dish and spoon.
- Encourage finger licking by gently guiding hands to mouths. Slow the pace down towards the end of the meal and give the babies time to dabble and make marks with their fingers on their plate.
- Over the next few weeks, as the babies begin to show signs of feeding themselves, give them their own set of food, dish and spoon to interact with in parallel to your own and gradually put more of the meal into their own dish.

Let's talk!

Make mealtimes sociable by constantly interacting with and talking to the babies. Set the pace of feeding so that it feels right for them – each baby is different. Introduce the simple vocabulary associated with feeding, ask *One more, more banana? Look – all gone!* Provide support by holding up an item and asking, for example, *Juice now?* Challenge the babies by asking, *Where's your spoon? Juice or banana?* Observe what stage each baby has reached in terms of self-care.

Top tip

Make sure you continue to interact and encourage the babies when they become independent. Don't be tempted to leave them to it just yet!

Differentiation

Use a gentle hand-over-hand to guide younger babies feeling and exploring their food. You can also dab tasty food items on to fingertips to encourage the first steps towards finger feeding. Load the spoon up for older babies and then place it in their hands so that they can begin to lift it to their mouths independently. Guide their hands at the wrist or elbow if necessary.

Further ideas

- Try a dab-and-taste activity, offering the older babies different foods to dab fingers into and taste.

Mirror art

Age range: 8–20 months

This activity combines a mirror and messy play for some enjoyable learning opportunities.

Development matters

Explore and experiment with a range of media using whole body.

Respond to the different things said to them when in a familiar context with a special person.

Setting up

Mix up some finger paints or poster paints really thickly ready for finger painting. You need a mirror on the wall at the children's height (ensure this is completely safe) and spread a plastic sheet beneath it. Make sure you have plenty of aprons, hand-washing bowls, cloths and towels to hand.

Getting started

- Show one or two children the mirror and make dabs on to the surface with your finger paints. Admire the effect with the children and encourage them to have a go. Use your fingers to make lines, dabs and circular movements and encourage the children to imitate and experiment.
- Try palm prints and hand wipes too. Draw the children's attention to the marks and patterns they are making, then sit back and observe whether they are repeated or developed. Now introduce some print blocks and the rollers and, after showing the children how to use them, allow them to experiment.
- Make hand-washing a sociable time together and take your time as you talk and clean yourselves up together. These times can often be as full of learning opportunities as the activities themselves.

Let's talk!

Provide support by giving a simple commentary about the children's actions and the colours: *Ruben is painting, Now the yellow, I'm painting your smile!* Provide extension by offering choices and naming colours and simple concepts, *Do you want the red paint now? Here's the roller to try. Let's wash hands – one hand, two hands.* As you begin to play together, try giving the children simple instructions and noting whether they respond to your words alone or whether they need to be shown what to do.

Top tip

Using a mirror helps the children feel valued and part of the group as they can see each other and watch you encourage them as they play. Don't be afraid to sit back and watch as they become involved in and pensive about what they are doing.

Differentiation

Keep this simple by just using fingers and hands at first. Challenge children by asking them to 'help' you to wipe the mirror clean afterwards. Expect more of a mess than before and enjoy experimenting with the colours as they blend and run together.

Further ideas

- Enjoy this activity outside as well by painting on a low-level window. Involve children on each side of the glass and observe their interactions.

Jelly wobble

Age range: 8–20 months

Have fun exploring the wonderful texture of jelly together – and expect plenty of mess!

Development matters
Enjoy making noises or movements spontaneously.

Setting up

Find a new washing-up bowl or large plastic mixing bowl. Make up several packs of jelly (opt for healthier versions). Allow it to cool and when it's almost ready to set, add it to the plastic bowl. If you are really clever, you can melt different colours of jelly in stages and add it to your bowl in stripy layers. Cover the jelly until you are ready to play with it. Spread out a protective plastic sheet on the floor – outside on a warm day is idea. Have hand-washing bowls and towels handy. Check for any allergies since some jelly will inevitably be tasted.

Getting started

- Enjoy handling the jelly as you poke it and squeeze it between your fingers. Encourage the children to join in and share the fun and to make plenty of noise as they vocalise and laugh together.
- After a while, the jelly will develop quite a gloopy, runny consistency which is equally fun to dabble in and explore. Enjoy the rhyme:

  Jelly on a plate,
  Jelly on a plate,
  Wibble wobble,
  Wibble wobble,
  Jelly on a plate

  as you talk and play together. Enjoy the sociable time of cleaning yourselves up afterwards.

Let's talk!

Offer support by introducing words that describe the changes that the children will experience as they handle the jelly: *it's sticky/runny/squelchy/red.* Make this more challenging by making up new versions of the rhyme to enjoy – *Jelly on a spoon, Jelly in my tum* or even *Jelly on Kieron* (and so on). Observe how the children respond to the new medium and the vocalisations that they use.

Top tip

Some children become easily distressed if they become messy (sometimes because of people's reactions to them in the past). Introduce messy play such as this gradually and keep your voice encouraging as the children spend short times exploring how messy materials feel.

Differentiation

Keep this simple by introducing the jelly play in smaller bowls on a high-chair tray. Make the activity more challenging by introducing tools to play with the jelly, such as spoons and containers.

Further ideas

- Think of different ways to develop your sand and water tray by using different media to play with that are safe for young children to explore. Jelly is a wonderful starting point but you can also try dry ingredients or even custard!

Messy play day

Age range: 16–26 months

Here is an idea for planning a 'messy play day' as a way of getting the children to explore the world around them.

Setting up

Plan this activity ahead by setting out a number of messy play activities indoors and out. Try adding gentle baby bubble bath to the water tray (check for allergies), add glitter to the finger paints, add tubes and funnels to the sand tray and make swirly colours for your play dough. Provide opportunities for children to stick collage materials to boxes and packages. You'll need one adult to every two children.

Getting started

- Towards the beginning of your session, get everyone wrapped up in aprons or suitable clothing and hold hands with one or two of the children. Start a chant as you move around the room – for example, *'Hey ho, hey ho, it's off to play we go'*. Visit the first messy play area and enjoy the effects.
- Each pair of children can visit a different messy play area with their adult. As soon as the children have explored that area fairly briefly, start your chant and move on to another area.
- Stop to talk to other children as you pass each other and share what you have been up to. Keep the structured part of the activity short so that the children remain interested. Once the children have tried a sample of activities, offer them choices and support them as they begin to develop preferences. Then leave the activities out and support the children as they explore them in more depth.

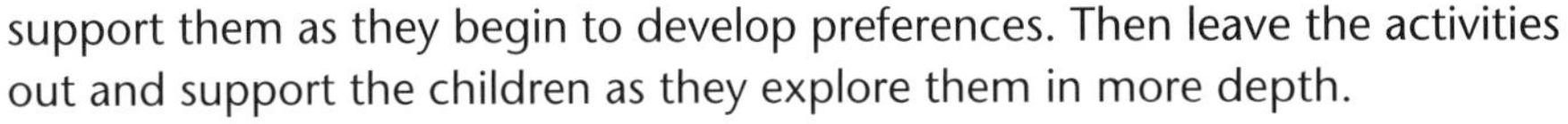

Let's talk!

Ask, *Do you like the sticking or the sand best? What shall we do now?* Support children by commenting on their actions, *You've been in the paint!* Make your language more challenging by asking the children about the past or the future. *What did you do before?* Observe children repeating sequences of actions as they develop their play in each of the messy play areas. Note their choices and preferences.

Top tip

Offering choices is one way in which you can encourage the children's participation and sense of belonging. However, being able to make genuine choices depends on their knowing 'what's on the menu' so occasionally it is a good idea to encourage children to 'have a go' at something new.

Differentiation

Keep this simple by encouraging a child to try one new messy play activity per session. Extend this by helping the children plan ahead and review where they have been and what they have done.

Further ideas

- Take photos of the various activities and use these to help children talk about their experiences and make choices for future sessions.

Mud pies

Age range: 16–26 months

Remember mud pies? You will never prevent young children from wanting to mix water with dry sand – so why not give in?

Setting up

Set up this activity on a hard area outside. Fill one bowl (washing-up bowls work well) half full with dry sand and another (which you will probably need to keep refilling) half full of water. Leave two or three other bowls empty and place a selection of tools and containers on the ground nearby. Include cups, small buckets, scoops, toy rakes and plastic boxes.

LEARNING AND DEVELOPMENT

Development matters

Sometimes focus their enquiries on particular features or processes.

Use tools and materials for particular purposes.

Getting started

- At first, simply sit back and watch what the children do. If necessary, step in and begin to make your own mixture of dry sand and water. Model how to use some of the tools and then step back again to support the children as they develop their own explorations and make their own discoveries.
- Help the children notice differences as the sand becomes wetter and behaves in a new way. Leave your mixtures and shapes to evaporate in the sun and revisit later to see what has happened next.

Let's talk!

Introduce new action-word vocabulary such as *mix, stir, poke, pat* and new describing words such as *dry, wet, stiff, runny, muddy.* Provide support by offering a simple commentary as the children explore, *Jamie is mixing.* Make this challenging by asking, *What does it feel like?* Jot down some of the children's language as they mix and explore and note how they begin to initiate new ideas of their own and sustain their concentration.

Top tip

Young children are driven to sensory play as a natural way of making sense of their worlds. Encourage them to focus on what they can see and feel as they play. Point out to them how the materials change as they try different actions. Stand back occasionally to encourage the children to take the initiative themselves.

Differentiation

Simplify the activity by offering a water bottle, a wooden spoon and a bowl of dry sand to play with at first. Extend the activity by moulding sand sculptures decorated with shells and other collage materials.

Further ideas

- Play together with sand and water on a large shallow tray and create miniature worlds and landscapes together, such as seasides for little people or tracks for racers.

Buried treasure

Age range: 22–36 months

Sand play can become so much more if you create an interesting theme around it.

Development matters

Begin to make-believe by pretending.

Use language as a powerful means of widening contacts, sharing feelings, experiences and thoughts.

Setting up

Collect about 20 interesting 'treasure items' to bury in your sand tray such as large 'gold' coins, plastic beads or cups. Make sure they are appropriate items that the children have not seen before and which will capture their interest. Set up the sand tray outside and bury half the items deep in the sand. Say nothing to the children.

Getting started

- Go outside with the children and encourage them to play with your usual resources. As they play, keep an eye on the sand tray so that you can hover at the right moment!
- As soon as one of the children finds the 'treasure', make a big fuss and pretend to be really surprised! At this point, encourage the finder to go and fetch another child to share the surprise with.
- As the activity progresses and more and more 'surprises' are found, encourage the children to communicate their findings with each other and spread the news. Keep some of the treasure in reserve so that there is plenty to be found by late arrivals.
- Repeat the activity for several sessions, using a different theme each time – buried treasure, dinosaurs, cars and trucks, crayons and so on. Extend the play by helping the theme to develop, for example, by creating a dinosaur park in the sand or making tracks for the cars.

Let's talk!

Help the children to find the words and gestures to communicate with each other about what they have found. Offer support by providing any new vocabulary needed, *Can you find any jewels?* Challenge the children by encouraging them to use their imaginations, *Do you think pirates have been here? What were they doing?*

Top tip

Support a child's first efforts at communication so that they gain confidence in being able to engage with other children. Sometimes this involves being there to act as a 'channel' of communication between them and to interpret their intentions. This is especially important for children who speak various languages.

Differentiation

Encourage children who need support to play in pairs, taking turns as one hides a toy for another to find. Extend the idea with imaginary play, for example, working with one group of 'pirates' to bury treasure for others to find.

Further ideas

- Choose a theme, such as dinosaurs, and hide a set in different locations of the outdoor space and playroom to be discovered by the children throughout the session.

Splat pictures

Age range: 22–36 months

Let gravity be your helper as you enjoy creating artwork from above!

Development matters

Begin to combine movement, materials, media or marks.

Are curious and interested in making things happen.

Setting up

Use your wet play area or outdoor hard surface and cover the ground with a protective plastic sheet. Place a sturdy child-height chair on to the sheet with a low table beside it. Mix up some paints to an extra thick consistency – ask the children to help you. Arrange some collage materials (pasta shapes, sparkly pieces, coloured feathers, tissue paper shapes and so on) in pots around the table to look appealing. Have some bowls and large sheets of fairly stiff art paper in different colours and shapes nearby.

Getting started

- Encourage the children in turn to come to the table and create their own mixture of paint and collage materials in their individual bowl. Enjoy the changes and the process as the children choose more ingredients for their 'soup'. Now help the children to choose a piece of paper and lay it on the plastic sheet behind the chair.
- Help each child to climb steadily and safely on to the chair and kneel against the back. Hold the bowl as the child spoons dollops of mixture over the edge and on to the paper. Watch and enjoy the effects created!

Let's talk!

By all means make suggestions, but also stand back to allow the children to make and experiment with their own choices as they make their mixtures. Offer support by adding a simple commentary to describe their choices, *What a shiny one! I like the yellow feathers!* Provide challenge by wondering, *What would happen if …?* Observe how carefully each child thinks about their mixture and the effects created on the paper. What do they say to you? What do they do the next time?

Top tip

Some children (and parents) might need your reassurance that it is acceptable to 'make a mess' (as they might see it). Explain to any parents that children need to experiment and explore and that they are also being little scientists as they discover how things fall and land.

Differentiation

Keep this simple by just enjoying the mixing part of this activity. Make the activity more challenging by encouraging children to plan the effects they are going to create with gravity – what would look really amazing?

Further ideas

- Mount paper on a wall above your sheet and observe what happens when you apply your mixture to the top and it slithers down the sheet.

What's outside? Cherry blossom

Age range: 0–11 months

Use natural resources to start introducing babies to the world around them.

Development matters

Use movement and sensory exploration to connect with their immediate environment.

Setting up

Choose your moment. These ideas are based on making the most of your natural outdoor environment. There may be a light breeze and the cherry blossom is beginning to float down. Perhaps the first autumn leaves are beginning to change colour and to fall. You may have a light shower with sunshine and rainbow colours shining through. In winter there may have been a light snowfall and sparkly frost.

Getting started

- Dress the babies appropriately for the outside and take them out in their buggies or prams. Pause to enjoy the sights and sounds. Younger babies might be content to lie in their prams and kick beneath a tree or enjoy a stroll in their buggies through the puddles as you push them along.
- Create your own outdoor spectacle by suspending a series of eye-catching objects beneath a clothes line just above adult height across your outdoor space. Include items such as leaves, blossomed twigs, fluttering ribbons and sparkly discs. Park the babies where they can enjoy the sights as these turn and flutter in the breeze. You could involve the older children in creating this for the babies.

Let's talk!

Talk gently to the babies as you come across new sights and sounds. Provide support by using your voice to engage their attention, to reassure and to help the babies stay alert. Challenge by saying, for example, *Look at the leaves.* Observe whether the babies' attention is held yet by the sights and sounds around them and how each of them responds.

Top tip

Many great-grandmothers used to place a pram beneath an apple blossom tree for the baby to lie, kick happily or fall asleep! By introducing the outdoor environment early, you are helping the children to feel familiar with it, which may encourage them to explore and play there actively when they are older.

Differentiation

Younger babies will enjoy being moved in their buggies or held as you explore the outdoor world together. Older babies might enjoy a toddle or a kick in the leaves with you if you hold them.

Further ideas

- Suspend ribbons from the branches of a tree or from a wire fence for the children to watch. Wind chimes make a soft sound for babies to listen to if the breeze is gentle.

The watching window

Age range: 0–11 months

Create a special outdoor space that can also be enjoyed indoors through a window.

Development matters

Learn by observation about actions and their effects.

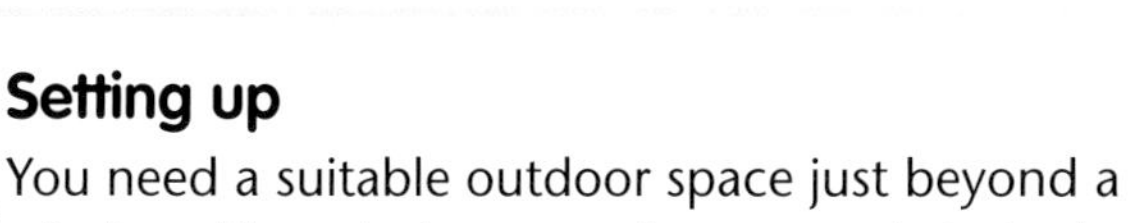

Setting up

You need a suitable outdoor space just beyond a window. The window you choose needs to be low and ideally to have a low window seat or ledge just inside it for older babies to stand up against and 'cruise' along.

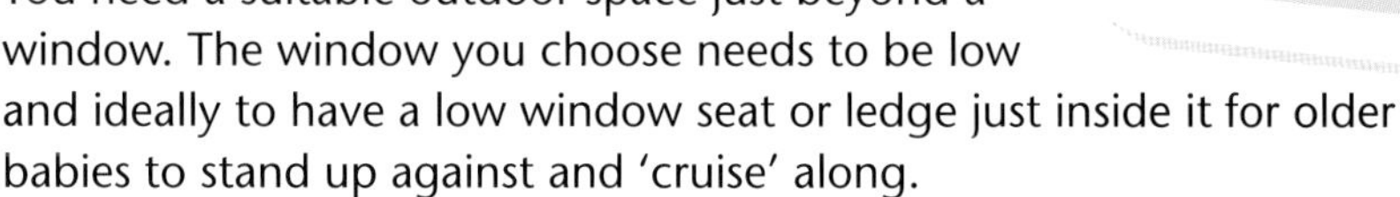

Getting started

- Select your outdoor area. The idea is to create a space that can be easily viewed through a window and which is full of interesting sights, such as a brightly painted wall, some twisting wind chimes and mobiles, bright flowers or shrubs and interesting safe surfaces to feel or crawl across. Plan and create this over a period of time, involving some of the older children. Plant flowers and plants that are attractive all year round and safe for children – your local garden centre should be able to advise you.
- Spend time outside enjoying your space, but also visit it 'through the window' so that you can enjoy it from within. Some watching windows might overlook busy roads and pavements which would provide you with plenty to observe and talk about. When one of the babies is outdoors enjoying the space with an adult and you are still indoors, draw other babies' attention to what is going on outside the window. Hold them close so they can watch.
- When one of you is outside, try catching the attention of the children indoors through the window.

Let's talk!

Even with young babies, you can begin to talk gently about what you see and what is happening, *Look, Leon is smelling the flowers*. Provide support by echoing back the sounds that they make to you. Challenge the babies by using your gestures, voice and general air of expectation to offer them the choice to go outside and then oblige, *Shall we go and join Leon? Yes?* Observe the children's own signals for asking to go out or in and also how they begin to anticipate what they will see through the window.

Top tip

When planning your outdoor spaces, always plan for quiet, restful areas as well as lively, active ones. This allows you to spend quiet times with each child and build up your positive relationship with them.

Differentiation

Younger babies will enjoy watching if you attract their attention with movement and voice as well as sights and sounds. For babies needing more challenge, play 'hide and seek' through the window as you disappear and reappear into sight.

Further ideas

- This 'watching window' could also be the window at which parents wave goodbye to the babies.

Picnic time

Age range: 8–20 months

Picnics create many learning opportunities and can take place anytime, anywhere.

> **Development matters**
> Begin to indicate own needs, for example, by pointing.

Setting up

Gather together some healthy food options to prepare a picnic.

Getting started

- Explain to the children that you are all going on a picnic. Prepare some healthy finger snacks by, for example, cutting bananas into slices, cubing cheese, halving strawberries, baking miniature fairy cakes and cutting bread-and-spread fingers. Aim for a range of foods to suit all tastes, representing the families and communities you work with. Be aware of any allergies the children might have. Place each food item in a different small container.
- Now make a grand occasion of dressing appropriately, choosing the toys you will take outside and 'packing' the food containers into baskets. When you are all ready, set off on your expedition, helping the children to toddle or be carried towards your destination outside. Do not go directly there – use a circuitous route and enjoy the journey!
- Decide where you will 'camp' and spread out a groundsheet and rug. Open the containers together and place each food item in a different bowl on the rug. Support the children as they share the snacks and point to what they would like to taste next.

Let's talk!

Offer the children food choices by holding up each item and asking, *Would you like a strawberry or some banana?* Provide support by naming the items as you pass them, *Here's a sandwich, Have some cheese*. Challenge the children by asking, *What would you like next?* Praise the children for sharing and passing the containers to each other, even though they are too young to understand this concept yet. Observe whether the children can use pointing to indicate their choices and needs.

Top tip

Make snack and mealtimes sociable, enjoyable and relaxed occasions. There is no reason why these should always be indoors. Look for chances to make outdoor snack times a regular part of your sessions, whenever the weather allows.

Differentiation

Make this simpler by offering a choice of finger snacks on one dish for the children to reach for and try. Extend the idea by involving the children in the food preparation at whatever level is appropriate.

Further ideas

- Involve the soft toys too and make yourselves an outdoor den using sheets or enormous cardboard boxes. If the weather is unkind, enjoy your picnic indoors but in a different room, and try again another day.

Rain and shine

Age range: 8–20 months

Rainy days and sunshine provide plenty of inspiration for rhymes and songs.

Development matters

As they pull to stand and become more mobile, the scope of babies' investigations widens.

Develop an awareness of number names through their enjoyment of action rhymes and songs that relate to their experience of numbers.

Setting up

A 'watching window' (see page 27) would be useful. Prepare four large cards with simple illustrations of sunshine, rain, wind and clouds.

Getting started

- Wait for a day when the weather is distinctive and obvious for all to observe – bright sunshine perhaps, or heavy rainfall. Draw the children's attention to the weather as they look through the window.
- Hold up a big card to represent the weather today. If the weather is suitable, move outside for some songs – if not, stay indoors and gather on your song mat. Here are some weather chants to enjoy together (chant them like a rap):

  Pitter pat, what was that?
  Three fat raindrops on my hat!
  One, two, three!

  Sunshine, sunshine on my nose
  Sunshine, sunshine on my toes
  Sunshine, sunshine on my head
  Goodbye sunshine, time for bed!

  Pause to emphasise counting (as you clap your hands) and body parts (as you point to them in turn).

Let's talk!

Say, *Look at the sunshine! It's raining today!* Provide support by using simple words to describe what the weather is doing. As you dress the children ready to go outside, explain that they need to be warm and so on. Challenge by asking, *What do you need to wear?* Observe how the children begin to notice the weather and how they change what they are doing in the light of this.

Top tip

Try not to describe one particular type of weather as 'bad' – we live in many weathers and need to find contentment in all of them! Use your encouragement and support to make all weathers interesting and enjoyable.

Differentiation

Support children while they enjoy simply watching the rain trickle down the window or tracing patterns with their fingers on to the window's condensation on a cold day. Challenge children to select the picture card that matches the weather.

Further ideas

- See if the children can spot their shadows if you move in front of or wave arms against a sunny wall.

Outdoor clothes

Age range: 16–26 months

Outdoor clothing gives you lots of opportunities for talking about the outdoors and developing independence.

Development matters

LEARNING AND DEVELOPMENT

Begin to learn that some things are theirs, some things are shared and some things belong to other people.

Show a desire to help with dress and hygiene routines.

Setting up

Gather together the children's usual selection of outdoor clothing and equipment, for example, boots, hats, jackets, gloves and scarves.

Getting started

- Work with two children at a time. Before they go outside to play, visit the window and have a look at the weather. Go together to choose all the clothing items that they will need.
- Spread out the clothes on a mat with both the children's items mixed together. Take it in turns to put on boots, coats, gloves and so on. At each stage, pause to help the children find their own items of clothing and encourage them to assist you by holding up feet, holding out hands, zipping up and so on.
- Enjoy your outdoor play time together and then spend the same amount of time undressing together at the end. Again, encourage the children as they try to remove their own boots, gloves and hats.

Let's talk!

Once you have looked outside, talk about what you need to wear and what you need to do first. Support the children by asking them, *Can you find your boots?* Challenge them by asking them to identify or name body parts as you help them to dress and undress. *Where are your feet?* Observe exactly how much the children can do by themselves and at what stage they need help. In this way you can provide exactly the right amount of help and encouragement for each child.

POSITIVE RELATIONSHIPS

Top tip

Praise the children warmly when they manage dressing or undressing items 'all by themselves'. At first, make sure you provide the same amount of attention when the child is dressing independently as if you were dressing the child yourself – that way, they will enjoy showing off their new-found independence to you.

Differentiation

Break the dressing skills down into steps – which steps does the child find easy (such as holding out hands to have gloves put on) and which hard (like pushing fingers in). Use hand-over-hand to teach those steps that the children cannot yet manage. Make the activity more challenging by making the group larger so that there is a wider selection of items.

Further ideas

- Have a selection of everyday outdoor clothing as part of your regular dressing-up box. Include flashy sunglasses and shiny rain-hats for pretending games.

Out and about

Age range: 16–26 months

Here are some ideas for the next time that you are planning an outing or special trip with the children.

Development matters

Show interest in stories, songs and rhymes.

Sometimes focus their enquiries on particular features or processes.

Setting up

Select a favourite soft toy or puppet from your setting.

Getting started

- Think carefully about where you would like to take the children and start your usual preparations and notification letters to parents. One of you should visit your proposed destination first.
- Take photos of 'Big Ted' at each stage of the journey, starting with getting ready to leave and then, for example, catching the mini-bus. Think about each event or feature that the children will experience and photograph Big Ted in that situation. Make a point of capturing the parts that will interest and intrigue the children, such as the donkey ride at the children's farm or the puppet show at the leisure centre.
- When the photos are printed, mount them in a large scrap book, add a title (such as 'Big Ted's Trip to the Farm') and a small amount of text to help your colleagues ('This is Big Ted on the swings'). Use Big Ted to share the book with the children, one or two at a time, as an introduction to your forthcoming outing.

Let's talk!

As you take the children through your book, talk about where Big Ted went, what he did there and what he saw. Keep it simple by asking, *Who's this? What's this?* Challenge the children to take an interest and to talk about what they would like to do on the trip. *Where would you like to go? What would you like to do?* Observe how easily each child can make the link between your book and the future plans – do they know what to expect?

Top tip

Some children feel a lot more confident about facing new situations if they have some idea in advance about what to expect there. Less confident children can hold hands with Big Ted, who has seen it all before!

Differentiation

Keep this simple by using only three or four photos and show them to the children once more during the actual outing. Make the activity more challenging by involving one or two of the children in your pre-visit.

Further ideas

- Use the photos to offer choices to the children about what they would like to do on their outing. You might also offer them a choice of two or three venues and act on their preferences based on their responses to the photos.

The great outdoors

Age range: 22–36 months

Create your own outdoor adventure and nature area in your regular outdoor space.

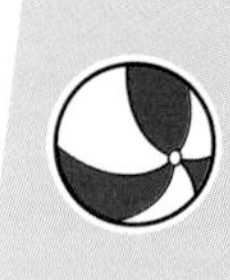

Development matters

Gradually gain control of their whole bodies and are becoming aware of how to negotiate the space and objects around them.

Setting up

Plan well ahead and spend a few weeks converting your outdoor space.

Getting started

- During autumn, section off a corner of your outdoor space with a plank of wood and fill behind with soil, dead leaves and old bark. Leave this cordoned off from the children until it has had the chance to develop into a beetle bank.
- Mount nesting boxes in good time for spring, high up and sheltered by any overhanging trees or hedges that you might have. Start to enjoy a bird table all year round by scattering crumbs, hanging baskets or strings of monkey nuts and suspending bird feeders full of mixed grains and seeds. Place it where the children can observe the birds through a window.
- Plant sturdy flower pots with wild grasses and flowers and keep them watered with the help of the children. Add pots of flowering plants such as buddleias to attract the insects.
- By summer time, you should have a wild area to explore and ramble in together. Arrange the pots so that the children have to negotiate their movement carefully and take their time enjoying all the sights and sounds around them.

Let's talk!

Involve the children in as much of the process as possible, especially feeding the birds and watering the pots. Talk about what you are doing. Provide support by pointing out all the interesting features of your nature ramble and use the opportunity to teach the children new vocabulary, such as *beetle, robin, bee, daisy*. Challenge the children by encouraging them to ask you questions and find out more. Observe the children's responses to what they see.

Top tip

Some children are very frightened of insects and small creatures, often because of the reactions of adults around them. Always stay calm, allow certain children to keep their distance and show through your own reactions how interesting these creatures are. Allow children to watch through the window if need be.

Differentiation

Keep this simple by holding the child's hand as you walk around the area and provide a simple running commentary of what you see. Challenge children by involving them in the planning, setting up and maintenance of your wildlife area.

Further ideas

- Look at simple information books of wildlife creatures and plants found in your nature area.

Outside memories

Age range: 22–36 months

This activity uses photos to trigger and talk about personal memories of being outdoors.

Development matters
Recognise some special times in their lives and the lives of others.

Setting up

Ask parents to send in photos of family holidays. Create an album for each child, using loose-leaf transparent pockets and ring files (check for safety).

Getting started

- This activity works really well where families lend you photos. However, this will not always be possible so make sure you build up your own collection of outdoor photos over the child's time with you. In particular, capture special times which the child is more likely to remember and occasions such as outings or celebrations.
- Make time to sit down with each child one-to-one. Spread the photos out on the floor beside you and 'go with the child' as pictures are recognised, celebrated and commented on. Suggest that you make a book together and help the child select photos to go in this. For each photo, talk about the child's recollection of what was happening or who was there, keeping your language very simple and concrete.
- Decide on a short title or few words to go with each photo. By now, the child will probably be ready to move on to another activity and so you can finish putting the album together later in your own time.
- Share the finished product with the child plus one or two friends as you talk about the outdoor memories it contains.

Let's talk!

Though you should keep your language simple, begin to introduce the past tense: *That's when you were on holiday!* Provide support by saying, *Tell me about this picture.* Challenge the children by leaving gaps and spaces for them to think and express their own thoughts and ideas. Observe how easily the children can recognise past events and record samples of the language they use when commenting about them.

Top tip

Use your memory-sharing to help the children feel really positive about who they are and what they have done. Use specific praise, making it clear to the children what you are celebrating. Encourage them to let you know why they liked each photo chosen.

Differentiation

If a child finds question words difficult (such as *Who* or *What*) try sentence completion, *This is a ... or Leo was making a ...* Encourage children needing support to turn the pages of the book. Challenge others to relate short phrases for the captions.

Further ideas

- Keep a 'book' about each child in your book corner for the children to look at, share and talk about their friends and memories.

Colours and shapes Look closely

Age range: 0–11 months

Babies must learn to use their eyes and to make sense of what they see – here is one way to help.

Development matters

Show interest in toys and resources that incorporate technology.

Setting up

Collect a range of colourful moving toys including wind-up cot mobiles, push-button or pull-string propelling toys and electronic remote-control toys. These should be suitable for looking at rather than touching and handling.

Getting started

- For younger babies (four to eight weeks), the first stage is to teach them how to 'track' with their eyes, following a moving person or toy as it moves past their mid-line from left to right or right to left. Crouch about 20 to 25cm in front to catch their attention and move gently to the right and left as they follow you with their eyes or by turning their heads.
- As a next stage, hold a toy at their point of focus. Wave it and squeak it to attract their attention and then move it slowly from right to left and vice-versa as they turn to look.
- After this stage, the babies are ready to use their new tracking skills to follow all kinds of moveable toys, people and objects. Introduce your remote-control toys and share the pleasure as they appear from behind the furniture or disappear again. Pause between presentations to encourage the babies to look expectantly at you or to vocalise in order to indicate *More please!*

Let's talk!

To provide support in the early stages, encourage the babies gently with your voice as you move yourself or the toy across their line of vision. *Gemma – look at the ball.* Later see whether their attention is held just by looking and tracking without using your voice. At the end say, *Good girl! It's a ball!* Observe the stage at which their attentions are held by moving objects and how widely they can track these with their eyes. Notice the point at which they no longer look surprised when objects disappear and reappear again soon after.

Top tip

By using colour and movement you are making it pleasurable and interesting for babies to focus and track with their eyes. This helps them to make connections between the two sides of their brains and to lay down the links necessary for eye-hand coordination later on.

Differentiation

Keep this simple by encouraging babies to focus on musical wind-up cot mobiles. Challenge other babies to operate the push or pull propelling toys themselves and enjoy crawling or bottom-shuffling after them.

Further ideas

- Babies are fascinated by moving screen-savers on computers. Hold the babies up to look for a short time. Select ones which have slowly moving images tracking across the screen.

Yoo-hoo!

Age range: 0–11 months

Attract the babies' attention by using bold shapes with sharp, contrasting colours.

Development matters

Use movement and sensory exploration to connect with their immediate environment.

Develop an awareness of shape, form and texture as they encounter people and things in their environment.

Setting up

Make a set of brightly coloured soft shapes for the babies to reach for and handle. Cut out a square, circle, triangle and star from thick cardboard. These should measure about 30cm across. Lay these against brightly coloured washable fleecy fabrics and cut out the two of the same shape but 1cm larger. Each shape should be a different colour. Lay the two pieces of fabric for each shape together inside-out and start to stitch around the edges. Leave a gap, turn right-side-out and then lightly stuff each shape with non-toxic stuffing. Stitch up the remainder to create fleecy coloured shapes.

Getting started

- Make a game of hiding the shapes and then bringing them into view, sharing the babies' pleasure and surprise as they reappear. Encourage older babies to reach out and handle the shapes. These can be washed regularly when they have been mouthed.
- Keep the shapes out of general circulation by suspending them from the ceiling to twist and turn in the air.

Let's talk!

Use your voice to attract the babies' attention and keep this activity reassuring. To provide support, even though they are still very young, say the name of the shape as it appears, *Circle! Star! Square! Triangle!* To add challenge, leave a gap as you name the shape to encourage thinking, *It's a ...star!* Observe the babies' reactions as they grow older, when do they start to reach out and touch? When do they start to look for the hidden shapes?

Top tip

Vary which shape you present to the babies as their attention is caught for a short time by novelty. In fact, it is their response to novelty that lets you know that they are clever enough to spot the difference between the shapes and colours. Use your encouragement to keep this activity reassuring and interesting.

Differentiation

Simplify the idea by allowing the babies just to enjoy watching the shapes as they appear and reappear. Make this more challenging by encouraging babies to crawl or creep towards the attractive shapes as you lay them one at a time on the floor.

Further ideas

- Create a set of brightly coloured cardboard shapes and make these appear and disappear into boxes. At first, keep the same colour for each shape.

Rollaround

Age range: 8–20 months

Movement can be fun when you combine it with finding out about shapes that roll.

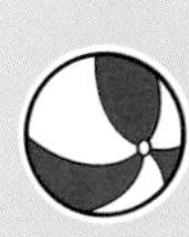

Development matters

Make strong and purposeful movements, often moving from the position in which they are placed.

Setting up

Lay out a large mat outside. Collect a selection of plastic balls of different sizes, from 10cm diameter to large inflatable beach-balls. Place some of the larger balls on the mat.

Getting started

- Ask one or two children to sit or stand on the mat at a short distance from the balls. Have fun creeping, crawling and rolling towards the balls. Encourage the children to push the balls away and move after them.
- Introduce some of the smaller balls and show the children how to let them drop from their hands and then crawl or toddle after them. Allow the children to develop their own play with the balls.
- Share some roly-poly rhymes together as you roll from side to side and enjoy the movement.

  Roly poly this way, roly poly back
  Roly poly ever so slowly, roly poly quick!
  Roly poly, bugs-in-a-rug, roly poly back
  Roly poly all-the-way-over and roly poly back!

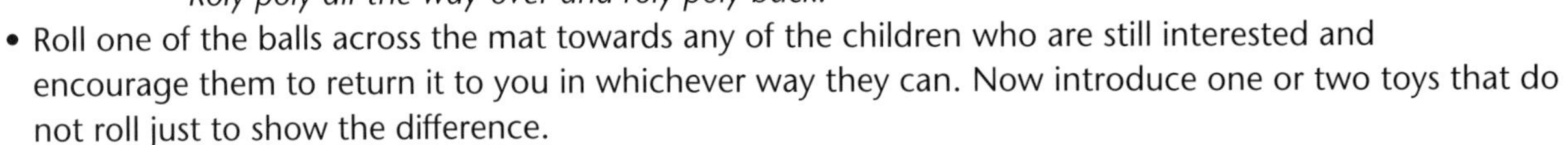

- Roll one of the balls across the mat towards any of the children who are still interested and encourage them to return it to you in whichever way they can. Now introduce one or two toys that do not roll just to show the difference.

Let's talk!

To provide support, introduce some of the vocabulary associated with colours and shapes – *Here's the red ball! It's round!* Challenge the children to complete simple actions linked to the shapes by saying, *Can you roll over?* Observe whether the children can link cause and effect by pushing, prodding or dropping a ball in order to move after it. Can they work out where it has gone and follow it?

Top tip

Balls are slippery objects and it takes persistence to catch up with them! Build up the children's confidence by under-inflating the beach balls slightly so that they are easier to manipulate, and by using soft sponge balls which do not roll too quickly. Praise and encourage all the time to enable them to feel good about their achievements and to build a positive relationship with them.

Differentiation

Keep this simple by using stuffed fabric balls with bells in (to hold attention) for children at an earlier stage. Challenge children to kick a ball if you steady them at the same time.

Further ideas

- Collect together a selection of your wheeled toys and turn the wheels with your fingers together, using some of the same vocabulary as you did earlier.

Surprise surprise!

Age range: 8–20 months

Colourful toys with a hidden surprise are excellent for helping children anticipate and link their actions with what happens next.

Setting up

Gather together all your surprise toys: pop-up toys, activity centres and jack-in-the-boxes. Select a teddy and a some baby clothes for the teddy to wear in a range of colours. Find a large box.

Development matters

Have a strong exploratory impulse.

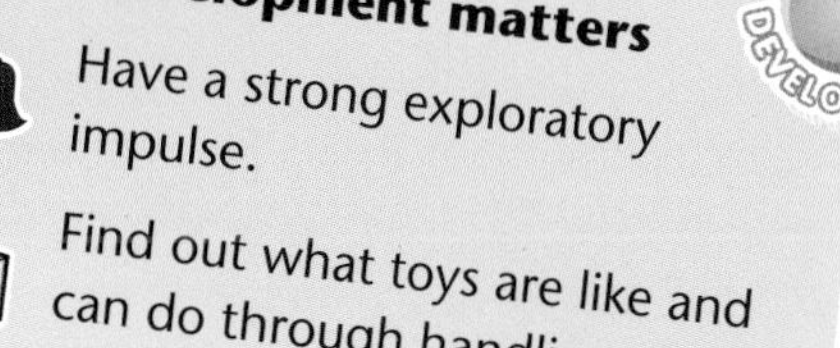

Find out what toys are like and can do through handling objects.

Getting started

- Start by introducing one of the surprise toys and showing the children how to make a simple action in order to obtain a surprise effect. Introduce several toys to keep up interest and leave these out to be explored.
- When the children have begun to make confident links between cause and effect, play this game together. Place Teddy and the baby clothes inside a very large cardboard box and put it in the centre of the floor.
- One of you should crouch inside the box as you dress Teddy up in one colour. The rest of you gather round to watch and build up the excitement as Teddy suddenly pops up into view wearing a particular colour.
- Repeat several times with Teddy popping up in a new colour each time! Try introducing an action that the children have to do in order to make Teddy appear, for example, all clapping hands or holding up a coloured block in order to decide on Teddy's next colour to wear.

Let's talk!

Ask, *What's going to happen? Do it again!* Keep this simple by saying, *Teddy up* and *Teddy down.* Challenge by asking, *What colour will Teddy wear next? Oh look – Teddy is wearing yellow!* Observe the children's reactions as Teddy appears. Note down evidence of the children showing clear signs of linking cause with effect in the way that they repeat their actions.

Top tip

Once you have established a positive relationship with each child, stay close to reassure when you first use surprise toys. The sudden effect can be alarming for some children, especially those with loud sounds.

Differentiation

Keep this simple by selecting activity centres with a simple push-knob action and use a gentle hand-over-hand to teach the action. Extend the idea by encouraging a child to squat in the box with you and a different child can pop up and surprise the others each time. This involves clever turn-taking.

Further ideas

- If the box is large enough, try a quick change (when you are out of view) into a different-coloured jumper and pop up yourself to surprise the children!

Same and different

Age range: 16–26 months

Colours and shapes are ideal for teaching sorting and matching.

Development matters
Categorise objects according to their properties.

Setting up

You need sheets of coloured foam (about 10cm thick) in red, green, blue and yellow. Make a set of shapes (for example, square, circle, triangle, star) out of each of the four colours. Each shape should be large enough for a small child to sit on. You will end up with 16 shapes.

Getting started

- Start by simply introducing the shapes to be played with generally in your setting. As you play, find natural opportunities to show the children that two colours or two shapes are the same or different.
- In time, the children may be able to move around, helping you to find shapes and colours that are the same (matching). As you tidy up together, engage the children in watching or helping you find the circles or find the red ones (sorting).
- When the children can sort and match the colours and shapes (and are a little older), start asking them to identify the colours and shapes by passing you the one you ask for. Later still, you might begin to hear the children spontaneously label the colours and shapes.

Let's talk!

Say, *Look! These are the same colour! That's the same shape! These are yellow. This is a triangle shape.* Provide support by asking simple questions, *Where's the yellow one? Can you find all the circles?* and then demonstrating the response. After a while, begin to challenge the children to *Find me another shape the same* or *Find me the other red one.* Keep the number of choices small at first. Observe when each child can match, sort, identify and name each simple shape and basic colour.

Top tip

Try to keep this activity natural and not to fire questions at the children. It is easy for a child to lose interest in colours and shapes if they never have an answer for you. Instead, create relaxed opportunities for them to match, sort and talk about colours and shapes spontaneously.

Differentiation

Children learn about colours by first matching them, then sorting them, then passing you the one you ask for and finally naming them. Keep this activity simple by putting out just four shapes that differ only in colour or only in shape. Make this more complex by challenging children to *Find the yellow one* or, to extend even further, *Find the blue star.*

Further ideas

- If you have made your shapes out of blocks of foam, cut them slightly smaller than their outlines to make a useful inset shape-board to play with on the floor.

Solid sort-out

Age range: 16–26 months

Start large-scale when you begin to introduce three-dimensional shapes for the children to explore.

Development matters

Are interested in pushing and pulling things, and begin to build structures.

Setting up

Collect a range of boxes and tape up the sides. Find some plastic jars or drums and glue the lids on. Seal the ends of strong cardboard rolls. This will give you a range of solid containers.

Getting started

- Turn your containers into brightly shaped blocks by painting them or wrapping them in brightly coloured wrapping paper (be prepared to re-wrap these again later as the wrapping paper itself will be enjoyed too!). Involve some of the children in this stage.
- Arrange the solid shapes on the ground outside and encourage the children to explore them. Intervene to model some suggested actions from time to time, such as pushing them, pulling them, lifting or stacking them.
- Challenge the children to sort and match the solid shapes. Try selecting the best shapes to build and stack with. Sit down to enjoy some shape songs and rhymes together.
- Take photos of what the children are doing and use these as a talking point afterwards.

Let's talk!

As the children play naturally, look for opportunities to name the shapes for them or provide a commentary on what they are doing in order to support them. *It's round. Here's a ball. Now here's a box.* Offer challenge by encouraging the children to work out, *Can you push it? Does it stack?* Observe whether the children have acquired an understanding of the properties of the solid shapes through the selections that they make to suit different purposes (for example, rolling or stacking).

Top tip

Starting 'large-scale' allows the children to interact more physically with the solid shapes and gain a multi-sensory idea of their properties: what they feel like, how they respond when you interact with them and so on. Try to use multi-sensory methods of teaching and supporting the children whenever you can, as it will help them make connections, feel successful and develop confidence.

Differentiation

Keep this simple by introducing a rolling game with round shapes or a stacking game with square shapes. Make the idea more challenging by asking the children to hunt for suitable solid shapes to fulfil the purpose they have in mind.

Further ideas

- Make a simple obstacle course out of large hollow containers and cartons for clambering through and experimenting with.

Shape hunt

Age range: 22–36 months

Here is an idea for using bright colours and bold shapes to build up children's memory skills at the same time as exploring their world.

Setting up

You need about 20 brightly coloured shapes, either from your selection of plastic toys or cut out from thick card. Select a range of interesting shapes and colours. Set this activity up before the children arrive. Attach thread to each shape and look around your play areas, indoors and out, for places to suspend the shapes so that they are out of reach of the children yet still in view (if you look carefully enough). Keep one or two of the shapes back in a basket.

Development matters

Use language as a powerful means of widening contacts, sharing feelings, experiences and thoughts.

Getting started

- Explain to the children that you have lost your shapes. Show them those remaining in your basket. Ask them to come and tell you if they see any. Then allow this activity to run throughout the course of the session, reminding the children from time to time that there are still some shapes missing.
- The idea is that the children will come and tell you if they spot a shape. As the shapes are out of reach, they will have to remember where the shape is and either use their words or actions to tell you what they have found and where. Follow their directions to the shape and retrieve it for your basket.

Let's talk!

Provide support by using their discoveries as natural opportunities to talk about what shape and colour they have found. *Here's the blue one. You've found a star!* For shapes which do not have a specific name, find other words to describe them, *The pointy one, The wiggly one* and so on. Challenge the children by asking, for example, *Where did you find your circle?* Note down how they can communicate to you what they have found.

Top tip

It is so important that young children feel successful in their early attempts to communicate. Always stay encouraging and interested, providing words for them and rephrasing when necessary. Give the children time to set their own pace when communicating with you and listen carefully with your whole attention.

Differentiation

Keep this activity simple by using just a few shapes well within the child's view. Make it more challenging by hiding the shapes out of view so that the children have to look behind doors, into corners or between leaves.

Further ideas

- Hide a brightly coloured ball and give the children spoken instructions explaining where to hunt for it.

The colour game

Age range: 22–36 months

Let a simple song add an extra dimension to learning about colours.

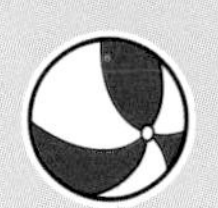

Development matters

Join in singing favourite songs.

Gradually gain control of their whole bodies and are becoming aware of how to negotiate the space and objects around them.

Setting up

Set out four coloured hoops (red, green, blue and yellow) in the middle of the floor outside. Keep matching coloured beanbags and bands or tabards for the children on one side in a basket.

Getting started

- Hold hands and dance around singing this song to the tune of 'Humpty Dumpty':

  Red or blue or yellow or green
  Red or blue or yellow or green
  Which are the colours that you have seen?
  Red or blue or yellow or green?

- Now let each child choose a beanbag from the basket and throw or carry it to the corresponding hoop. Sing the song again and repeat until all the beanbags are in their corresponding hoops. Gather them up again together. Now give out the bands or tabards (if you want to use them). Sing the song one more time and then put yourselves into the corresponding hoop, depending on your band, tabard or the main colour that you are wearing.
- Help the children get themselves into position and negotiate the tight space within the hoops as they all try to fit in with each other.

Let's talk!

Ask, *Where's the green hoop? This one is different.* Use the game to provide natural opportunities to name the colours for children who need support. Challenge children by asking, *What colour is your band? What colour does George have?* Notice whether the children can match or name the colours. Note down too whether they can throw with aim and negotiate their personal space in the hoops with each other.

Top tip

When you add physical action to learning, you make that learning more motivating, memorable and fun. If children are about to make wrong choices, simply lead them to the correct choice and reinforce the similarity – *Here's the yellow one – look!* Supporting learning is one of the main ways in which the EYFS suggests you can support positive relationships.

Differentiation

Make this activity easy by carrying beanbags to their corresponding hoops starting with a choice of just two colours. Challenge children by using coloured cards and introducing a wide range of coloured toys to match to the cards.

Further ideas

- Use the song at circle time and stop between each verse to look for a certain colour on yourselves, *Who is wearing red today?*

Materials Paper fun

Age range: 0–11 months

Encourage babies to enjoy feeling the texture of a range of different wrapping papers.

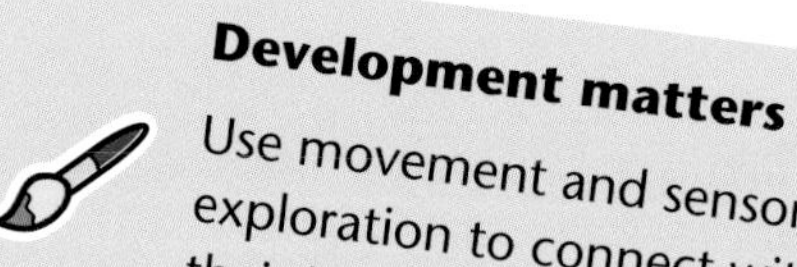

Setting up

Save wrapping paper – especially paper with bright colours or with crinkly, shiny textures. Look for high quality paper that does not tear easily.

Getting started

- Remove any old tabs of sticky tape or loose bits from the paper. Cut one or two holes in the centre of the larger pieces for you to peep through. Simply lay the babies on a mat indoors or outside (on a calm warm day) where they can see, feel, kick against or roll amongst the paper. Observe the babies for safety at all times in case they try to swallow pieces and remove loose sections of paper.
- Attract the babies' attention by crinkling the paper close to them. Demonstrate how the paper can be kicked against, scrunching loose balls of it within arm's or leg's reach of the babies and brushing these lightly against them.
- Cover your face with a sheet of paper and reappear again, sharing the fun. Lightly cover an older baby's face with tissue paper for them to pull off or shake away. Play 'peep-bo' as you do so.
- Encourage burrowing beneath the paper or covering up parts of yourselves loosely. Greet the babies as they come back into view. Older babies will enjoy feeling, ripping and scrunching up the paper – this is fine too, since they are finding out about the properties of the material they are exploring.

Let's talk!

Introduce some early position words as you play, *Up, down, gone.* Provide support by engaging the baby's attention and saying, *Where's Jess? Here she is! More?* Challenge babies by saying, *Look! Listen! Here you are!* as you watch, listen to and touch the paper. Observe how each baby interacts with the paper and look for actions that they are happy to repeat over and over again as they explore.

Top tip

As the babies play, imitate their actions and their vocalisations. With the older babies, this will lead to a very sociable two-way interaction in which you take turns at doing and talking.

Differentiation

With younger babies, softly crinkle tissue paper or metallic paper close by for them to turn towards. Older babies will enjoy unwrapping a loosely covered soft toy.

Further ideas

- Sheets of children's wrapping paper can make excellent posters for babies to look at above cots or changing mats.

Reach and swipe

Age range: 0–11 months

Some items just call out to be reached out for – here is an activity that makes the most of this.

Development matters

Use movement and senses to focus on, reach for and handle objects.

Reach out for, touch and begin to hold objects.

Setting up

You need a solid and safe frame that can stand over a play mat and from which you can suspend a selection of everyday objects. Adapt a 'baby gym' by removing the plastic toys.

Getting started

- Select three or four items to suspend from your frame so that the babies can reach for, swipe and explore a whole range of colours, textures and shapes. You might choose a wooden spoon, a bright pompom, a CD disc, a set of brightly coloured plastic measuring spoons, a toothbrush, a sponge, some soft toys, bells and so on. Avoid anything with small pieces that can be detached or swallowed.
- Select different items each session and attach them securely to the frame, so that they can be swiped at and reached for but not actually tugged off. You will have to judge the heights to hang them from, depending on the babies in your group.
- Stay close to the babies to encourage and model from time to time how to reach out for and swipe the items.

Let's talk!

To provide support, keep your language simple at this stage, echoing back the sounds that they make. Challenge older babies by introducing simple vocabulary, *There's the spoon! Here's Duck!* Observe the first signs of purposeful movement with arms or legs towards the items and note what attracted the babies to try this.

Top tip

The ability to grasp an object develops from these early attempts to reach and swipe, once the babies realise that closing fingers secures that item for further exploration. Your encouragement and your choice of attractive items will help them achieve this.

Differentiation

Keep this simple by suspending a large coloured pompom just above the baby to be knocked almost accidentally at first. The activity becomes more challenging when you arrange items on the frame that can not only be reached for but grasped and explored with safety.

Further ideas

- Suspend soft toys safely from a cot side for play and exploration on waking after a rest.

What's in the box?

Age range: 8–20 months

This game encourages both the children's exploration and anticipation using boxes and containers.

Development matters

Have some knowledge that things exist, even when out of sight.

Setting up

Collect a selection of three or four large boxes and containers that are safe for the children to explore and rummage in. Each should have a lid or flap that is easy to open. Collect the same number of large soft toys or colourful materials, such as a teddy bear, a plastic truck, a colourful scarf or an interesting shell.

Getting started

- This activity works well outside. Start very simply with one toy and one box. Make a game of hiding the toy in the box as you open the flap and find it again. Draw it out of the box slowly as you build up the excitement with your voice.
- Repeat two or three times until the child is beginning to anticipate and help. Now introduce the other boxes, each with a toy inside, and share the fun as you look inside each one and see what is there.
- By the end of this stage, everything will probably have been emptied! So take a favourite toy and 'hide' it (in the child's full view) in one of the boxes and see if the child can retrieve it. (Remove the other toys for the moment so that they do not distract.)
- At a later stage still, you can hide toys when the child is not looking and see if they can still be found. Leave the boxes and items out for the children to play with later in their own time.

Let's talk!

Use your talk to hold the children's attention and to sustain the play for longer. To offer support, use the child's name and say, *Look!* to engage and hold their attention. To add challenge, introduce the question sequence, *Where's the ...? Here's the ...!* Observe whether each child realises that a toy still exists even when it cannot be seen. Record evidence that the children are beginning to anticipate what is hidden in the box.

Top tip

Emptying out and putting in are favourite activities at this age. Use hiding and seeking games to allow children to build on this interest. Use your support to encourage the children to explore and find out even when things are not obvious; later this will develop into a healthy urge to ask questions.

Differentiation

This activity already works at many different levels of ability. Start with the first steps of the activity to keep it simple and build up to the more complex steps once the children's attention and curiosity can last longer. Add extra challenge by supporting the children in a simple game of 'hide and seek', either with people or hidden toys.

Further ideas

- Always keep some surprises hidden around the room in different containers to encourage searching, exploring and finding.

Mega art

Age range: 8–20 months

The children will enjoy creating a colourful wall mural by squirting paint!

LEARNING AND DEVELOPMENT

Development matters

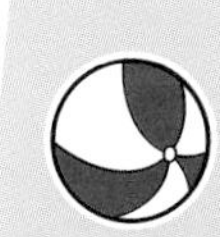

Enjoy the sensory experience of making marks in damp sand, paste or paint. This is particularly important for babies who have visual impairment.

Explore and experiment with a range of media using whole body.

Setting up

Fix a large sheet of paper firmly to a wall from ground level to 1.5m high, preferably outside. Place a large plastic sheet beneath it. You also need at least one adult for each child and another adult to help organise. Mix up some paints so that they are still quite runny and put each colour into a clean empty washing-up bottle. Experiment with the consistency. The idea is to get a good squirting consistency on to the vertical sheet which runs a little when it lands. Make a few experimental squirts to start off your mural.

Getting started

- Invite any interested children to put on aprons and approach what you are doing. Encourage them to watch or help you hold the bottles as you squirt colours carefully on to the paper. All the children should use the same sheet of paper to make this a communal event.
- Allow the children to move close and explore the paint with their hand and fingers as it makes shapes down the paper. Having one-to-one help will enable you to keep the children safe yet allow them to experiment fully.

Let's talk!

Introduce the colour names as you apply them. *Look at the red! Lovely purple! Help me with the yellow!* Provide support by adding a simple commentary as the children explore the colours and paints together. Challenge by saying, *Tell me about this.* Draw their attention to what each of them is doing. Observe the marks that they make and the way they interact with the materials.

Top tip

This activity encourages you to focus on *process* (interacting with the materials) rather than *product* (for example, making hand prints) and therefore allows you to encourage the children to feel motivated and successful. The praise and encouragement that this allows you to give will support the children in developing positive relationships with you and with each other.

Differentiation

This activity is useful for children with visual impairment because they need to feel what they cannot see when exploring paints. Keep it simple by exploring paints on the surface of a plastic tray. Challenge children to use a selection of large decorators' brushes, rollers and sponge blocks to apply the paint.

Further ideas

- Provide the children with washing-up mops to make wiping marks on your painted creation. This will add more texture and allow the children to experiment with mark-making.

Collage and chat

Age range: 16–26 months

This activity combines mirror and collage play with a special time together.

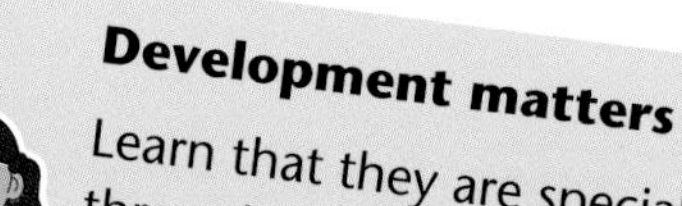

Development matters

Learn that they are special through the responses of adults to individual differences and similarities.

Are able to respond to simple requests and grasp meaning from context.

Setting up

This activity focuses on making children feel special and supporting their communication skills. It is therefore best to work individually with one child at a time. Try the activity out first on a small piece of glass to make sure that your glue really is washable! Secure a mirror at child height (ensure this is completely safe). Set up a tray of collage materials (such as sections of egg boxes, shapes cut from card or shiny paper – anything non-toxic and which cannot be swallowed) near to the mirror along with a saucer of washable glue.

Getting started

- When a child is ready to play with you, put on your usual overalls and encourage them to explore the collage materials. Use this as a special time to talk together, making the child feel important and successful. Participate wholeheartedly, laugh and make contact through physical play and hugs.
- Show the child how to dip an item of collage material into the saucer of glue and then apply it to the mirror. Then encourage them to copy you as you explain and model what you are doing. Continue to watch each other in the mirror and show that you value what the child is doing.
- Each child can add some collage in turn. When the time is right (and not before) you will be able to clean your mirror again!

Let's talk!

Run a commentary on what the child is doing to show that you are paying full attention. To provide support, make positive, *I like your ...* statements to show you value the child's play. Challenge the children by asking, *What did you do here?* Observe whether the children change what they are doing in the light of your demonstration or simple instructions.

Top tip

These ideas for positive support come from an approach known as 'supportive play' and help to strengthen relationships between carers and children. They also encourage children's unique individual development as the children make choices in their play and become competent learners.

Differentiation

Keep this simple by sharing special moments with the child around anything that has caught their personal interest. Make it more challenging by decorating the edge of your mirror so that you can still see each other clearly.

Further ideas

- Washable collage also works well on low-level windows to create a colourful display.

Fresh bread rolls

Age range: 16–26 months

Progress from play dough to the real thing in this cookery activity.

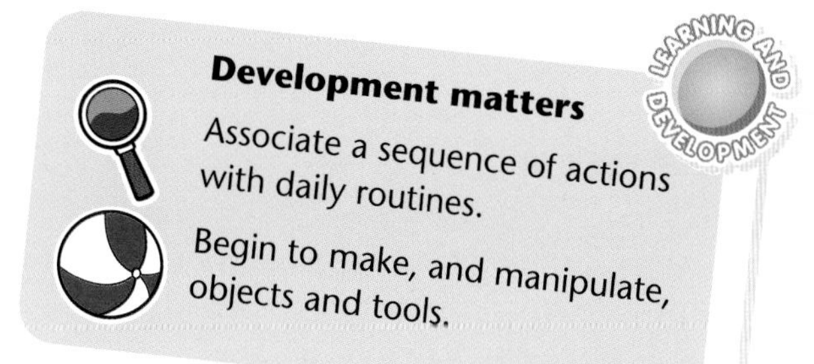

Setting up

Be aware of any allergies (especially gluten) and plan accordingly. Prepare your cookery area and gather together the ingredients and equipment you will need (see below).

Getting started

- Make sure that the children have been introduced to play dough over previous sessions and that they are already enjoying handling, squeezing, rolling or poking the dough.
- Place 700g of wholemeal/white mixed flour in a large bowl with two 7g sachets of fast-action (easy-blend) yeast; one heaped teaspoon of salt and one heaped teaspoon of unrefined sugar. Stir the ingredients until they are combined. The children should enjoy trying a brief stir between other activities.
- Make a well in the centre and add 425ml of warm water, stirring to form a sticky dough. Knead the dough for about 15 minutes until it is becoming smooth, elastic and easy to handle. Put the dough in a bowl, cover with a cloth and leave in a warm place for two hours until it doubles in size. Preheat the oven to 230°C/gas mark 8. Invite children to wash their hands and put on aprons. Show them how to punch the air out of the dough then give each child a small piece of the dough to pummel, shape, roll or poke with their fingers.
- Help the children lift their dough ball on to the baking sheet and paint it with milk. Make your own bread rolls for everyone with what is left. Leave for 20 minutes to prove then bake for 30 minutes. Cool and enjoy together later with a selection of spreads!

Let's talk!

To support the children, use simple language to explain that they are *baking* and that, this time, they are making real bread. *You're making bread! Can you roll/poke/make a ball like this?* Challenge children who need it by asking, *Does it feel sticky? Does it roll?* Observe whether the children can make the connection yet between the dough and the finished bread.

Top tip

Good cooking smells actually help us all feel more 'at home' and secure – use them to make the children feel settled and connected within your group.

Differentiation

Support children by stirring hand-over-hand. Make the activity more challenging by encouraging the children to shape their rolls in different ways.

Further ideas

- Try adding suitable toppings to your rolls, such as seeds, grated cheese, a honey glaze or crushed grains (be aware of allergies).

It's your choice

Age range: 22–36 months

Encourage the children to select their own materials for junk modelling.

Development matters
Begin to combine movement, materials or marks.

Setting up

- Collect used packaging and junk materials which are safe, appropriate and clean enough for the children to model with. Ask parents to contribute. As your junk material arrives, spend some time outside of the session to check it for appropriateness, hygiene and safety before storing it in a tub. Spread out a large plastic sheet on the floor (outside if the weather is right). Set up your usual sticking and modelling area adjacent to the sheet and materials.

Getting started

- Engage some of the children in unpacking the materials from the tub on to the sheet. Explore each item and use your ideas to encourage the children to think of what they might make with it. Move into model-making and sticking. Though the models will be very simple at this early age, the idea is to help the children select their own items rather than simply stick or paint with glue what is in front of them.
- The children may or may not decide what the model 'is' afterwards – that is not important. The point of the activity is to encourage exploring, selecting and doing – the process rather than the product.

Let's talk!

This looks like a TV! What a long box. Pass me that big one. These two look like a truck. Which one will you use? To provide support for children who need it, introduce describing words for the materials you explore together. *This one's red. This is hard.* Provide extension by talking about what items look like and what they might turn into. *What does this look like? What are you doing/making?* Note down evidence that the children can plan ahead at a simple level, selecting a piece of material and then incorporating it into a modelling or sticking activity.

Top tip

This activity helps children to make connections between one event (exploring a set of junk materials) and another (actually using these to model or stick with). Use your support and encouragement to help them concentrate and remember long enough to bridge this gap.

Differentiation

Keep the activity simple by limiting the amount of choice of junk materials. Make it more challenging by helping children who wish to make 'a something' to select suitable pieces for their model.

Further ideas

- Look for different ways of sorting out your junk materials together, such as boxes and tubs, big pieces and little pieces, food packages and other packages, square shapes and round shapes.